AF663087

Munshi Premchand

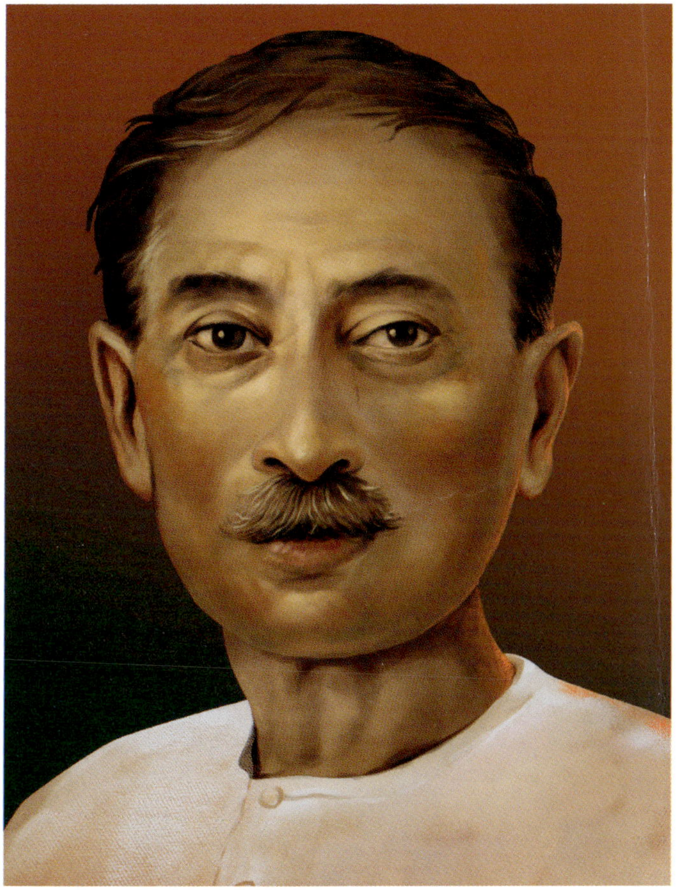

Om KIDZ
An imprint of Om Books International

First published in 2017 by

Om KIDZ
An imprint of Om Books International

Corporate & Editorial Office
A 12, Sector 64, Noida 201 301
Uttar Pradesh, India
Phone: +91 120 477 4100
Email: editorial@ombooks.com
Website: www.ombooksinternational.com

Sales Office
107, Ansari Road, Darya Ganj,
New Delhi 110 002, India
Phone: +91 11 4000 9000
Fax: +91 11 2327 8091
Email: sales@ombooks.com
Website: www.ombooks.com

© Om Books International 2017

ALL RIGHTS RESERVED. No part of this book may be reproduced or transmitted in any form by any means, electronic or mechanical, including photocopying and recording, or by any information storage and retrieval system, except as may be expressly permitted in writing by the publisher.

ISBN : 978-93-84225-22-3

Printed in India

10 9 8 7 6 5 4 3 2 1

Contents

Childhood & Early Life

Dhanpat Rai Srivastava, fondly known by his pseudonym, Munshi Premchand, was a pioneer of modern Hindustani literature. Among the most celebrated writers of the Indian subcontinent, Premchand was born on 31st July, 1880, in Lamati, a village near Benaras (present-day Varanasi). He was the fourth child of his parents. His father, Ajaib Lal, was a clerk in a post office and his mother, Anandi Devi, was a housewife.

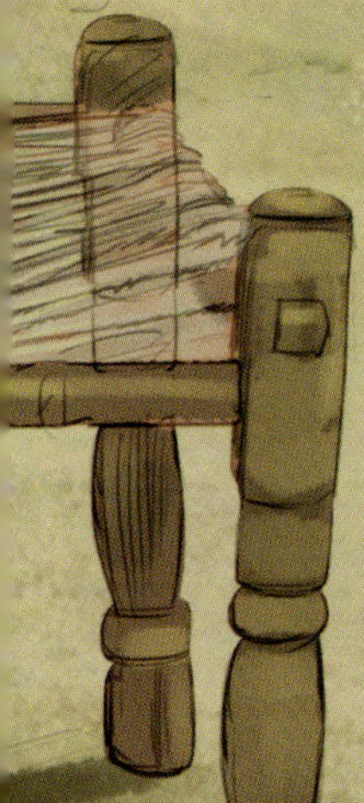

When he was seven years old, he was enrolled at a madarsa in Lalpur, located near Lamati, where under the tutelage of a Maulavi, he learnt Urdu and Persian. He was later enrolled in a missionary school, where he learnt English.

Premchand's mother passed away when he was seven. His grandmother took the responsibility of raising him, but soon after, she passed away too. His elder sister had already been married, his father was busy with work, and so, after his grandmother's death, Premchand felt isolated and lonely. Later, his father remarried. His stepmother was harsh, and had no affection for her stepson. Young Premchand's childhood was difficult and lonely, and so, he turned to books and soon became an avid reader.

In 1895, at the age of 15, he was forced to marry against his wish. The match was fixed by his maternal stepgrandfather. The girl was from a rich family and was older than Premchand.

The marriage didn't last long as Premchand found the girl quarrelsome, and it ended in 1899.

In 1897, when Premchand was 16, another tragedy struck him. He lost his father and was left with the responsibility of his stepmother and stepsiblings.

Times were tough and Premchand started tutoring a lawyer's child in Benares. This fetched him five rupees a month and he somehow managed to make ends meet. He stayed in a mud-cell above the lawyer's stables. Away from home, Premchand read a lot during these days.

Later, he also worked as an Assistant Master at a government school in Benaras. In 1902, he was appointed the headmaster of a school in Gorakhpur. After two years, he was sent to Kanpur as the Deputy Sub-Inspector of schools.

Beginning of Writing Career

Premchand stayed in Kanpur for around four years, from May 1905 to June 1909. It was in Kanpur that he met Daya Narain Nigam, the editor of a magazine called *Zamana*. He took a keen interest in political affairs during this period and often wrote on them. The writings were published in *Zamana*. In the evenings, there would be intense debate sessions with Nigam and other friends.

In 1905, he wrote an article for *Zamana* on Gopal Krishna Gokhale, a senior leader of the Indian National Congress.

He criticised Gokhale's methods for achieving political freedom. Instead, he advocated more extreme measures, like the ones adopted by Bal Gangadhar Tilak.

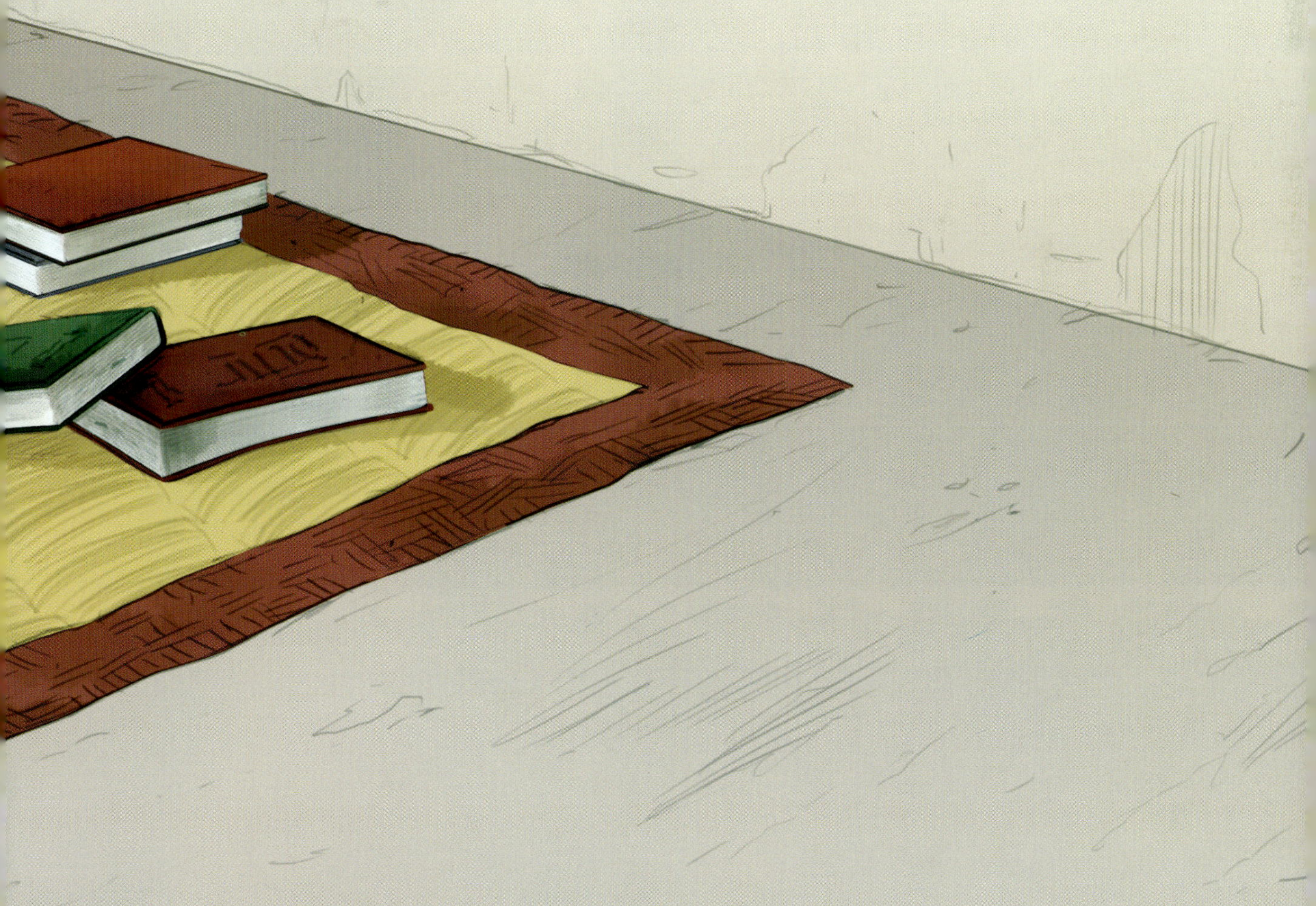

During his stay in Kanpur, Premchand would visit his village Lamati in his summer holidays. He never enjoyed his vacation, because the sultry weather was not conducive to writing.

In 1906, Premchand decided to remarry. His second wife Shivarani Devi was a child-widow and her father was a landlord. During this period, Widow remarriage was unheard of.

Marrying a widow was a radical step and Premchand faced a lot of social criticism for his decision. After his death, Shivarani Devi wrote a book on him, titled *Premchand Ghar Mein* (Premchand in the House).

From Nawab Rai to Premchand

Premchand was a voracious reader since childhood. After his mother's demise, he sought relief in reading. His love for books was such that he even worked with a book wholesaler once, just so he could read a lot of books.

In school, he was exposed to many works of fiction, including *The Mysteries of the Court of London,* George W.M. Reynolds' eight-volume work.

It was in Allahabad, where Premchand, the writer, was born. He started his literary career by penning short stories in Urdu. Sadly, his first literary work was never published

In the early days of his writing career, he wrote under the pseudonym 'Nawab Rai'. His first novel, *Asrar-e-Ma'abid* (The Mystery of God's Abode), revolved around the theme of corruption. The novel was serialised in an Urdu weekly, *Awaz-e-Khalk*, from October 1903 to February 1905.

Premchand's first story which got published was 'Duniya Ka Sabse Anmol Ratan' (The Most Precious Jewel in the World). This story was also featured in *Zamana* in 1907.

In the story, he stated: 'the most precious thing on Earth is the last drop of blood which is shed for the freedom of the country.'

زمانہ

In 1908, Premchand wrote five patriotic stories in a collection titled *Soz-e-Watan*. In 1909, Premchand was transferred to Mahoba, and later posted to Hamirpur as the Sub-Deputy Inspector of schools. He then fell victim to chronic dysentery, which later became the cause of his death.

Around this time, the British labelled *Soz-e-Watan* rebellious literature. According to the British, the collection of stories provoked Indians to fight for the nation.

The British collector of the Hamirpur District ordered a raid on Premchand's house, where around five hundred copies of *Soz-e-Watan* were burnt. Premchand was banned from writing anything without the permission of the authorities.

The pseudonym, Nawab Rai was of no use as he couldn't write according to his own creative and artistic desires. Dhanpat Rai changed his pseudonym from 'Nawab Rai' to 'Premchand.'

Success in Writing

In 1914, Premchand was transferred to the Basti district. By this time, he had established himself as a fiction writer in Urdu. But writing in Urdu was not monetarily rewarding. So, he started writing in Hindi.

His first Hindi story, 'Saut', was published in a magazine called *Saraswati*, in December 1915. In August 1916, when he was transferred to Gorakhpur, Premchand developed a friendship with the bookseller, Buddhi Lal. In exchange for selling exam guides at the school, Buddhi Lal would allow him to borrow novels to read.

Premchand was also an enthusiastic reader of classics in other languages, and translated several of these works in Hindi. His first Hindi short story collection, *Sapta Saroj*, was published in June 1917.

In 1919, Premchand's first major novel, *Seva Sadan*, was published in Hindi. It was originally written in Urdu, under the title *Bazaar-e-Husn*, but was first published in Hindi by a Calcutta-based publisher. Premchand was paid 450 rupees for his work.

The novel narrates the story of an unhappy housewife, who first becomes a courtesan, and then begins managing an orphanage for the young daughters of the courtesans. It was well received by critics, and helped Premchand gain wider recognition.

Most writers of those times wrote fantastical or mythological tales. Premchand was the one who introduced realism into Hindi literature, which was considered a revolutionary development at that time.

His stories dealt with social issues like dowry, poverty, corruption and zamindari. He was the first writer of the twentieth century to combine fiction with a social purpose.

Unlike other contemporary writers, his novels usually didn't feature a hero. A translator, novelist, story-writer, script-writer and dramatist, Premchand has been referred to as the 'Upanyas Samrat' by many Hindi writers.

Saraswati Press

Tragedy struck Premchand when he lost his youngest son to smallpox. After some time, Premchand himself fell ill. In this manner, his financial constraints kept increasing.

He was also fed up with his job as a teacher in government schools. He strongly wished to settle down and involve himself in publishing. In 1921, although physically unwell, after consulting with his wife, he decided to quit his government job of 21 years.

To make ends meet, he took up a job as an editor with a monthly newspaper, *Maryada*. But misfortune struck once again and he lost his job. After that, he was posted as the headmaster at Kashi Vidyapeeth, Benares.

In the year 1923, he established a printing press and publishing house in Benares, and named it 'Saraswati Press'.

Premchand was at his creative best and he wrote some of his most well-known stories like 'Shatranj ke Khiladi' and 'Sawa Ser Gehu'.

The year 1924 also saw the publication of Premchand's *Rang Bhoomi*, which features a blind beggar named Surdas as its tragic protagonist. The book received much appreciation from all quarters.

Some of his other significant works include *Nirmala*, a novel which explores how the dowry system functions in India. It was published in *Chand* magazine between 1925–1926, before it got published as a novel.

Another famous work of his is *Pratigya* (The Vow) that deals with the subject of widow remarriage.

हंस

In March 1930, Premchand launched a literary-political weekly magazine titled *Hans*, aimed at inspiring Indians to unite against the British rule. When the magazine failed to make a profit, Premchand started another magazine called *Jagaran*, which too, ran at a loss.

Premchand in Bombay

In 1934, Premchand arrived in Bombay. His financial situation was very dismal and hence, he decided to be a part of Hindi films. He accepted a scriptwriting job with the production house 'Ajanta Cinetone' with an annual salary of 8000 rupees.

He stayed in Dadar, and wrote the script for the film *Mazdoor*. The film, directed by Mohan Bhawnani, depicted the dismal conditions of workers. Premchand himself played a cameo role as the leader of workers in the film.

Since the film revolved around such a delicate issue, there were several problems during the release of the film. Though it managed to get a release in Lahore and Delhi, it was subsequently banned, after a mill workers' uprising was reported.

Ironically, the film ended up inspiring the workers of Premchand's own press in Benares to go on a strike, as they were not paid their salaries.

Sadly, the printing press where Premchand had invested his lifelong savings was running at a loss. His brother had also invested in it but it wasn't reaping any benefits.

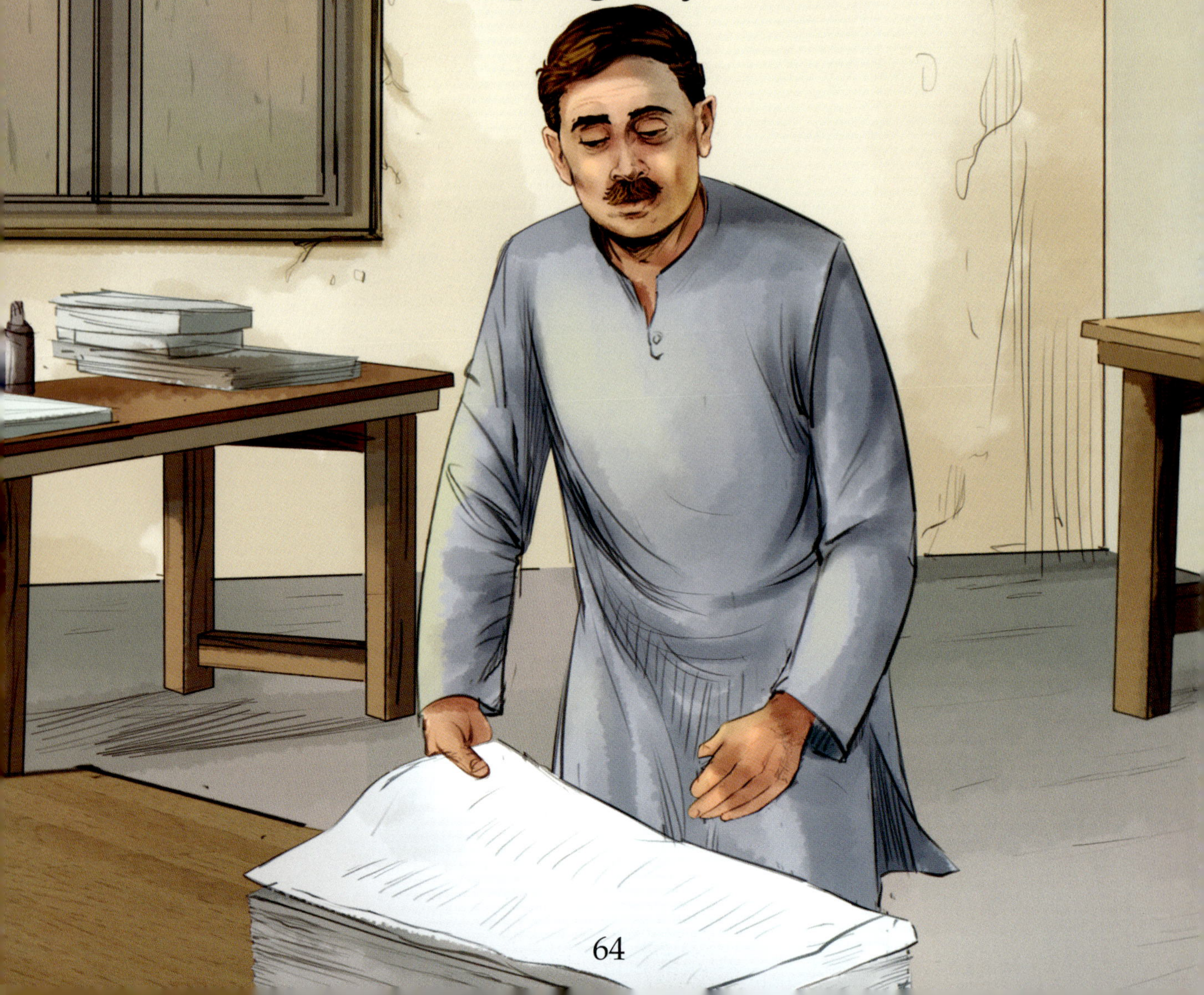

By 1934–35, Saraswati Press was under a heavy debt of 4,000 rupees, and Premchand had no choice, but to discontinue the publication of *Jagaran*.

Meanwhile, Premchand developed a dislike for the commercially oriented environment of the film industry and wished to return to Benares.

Last Days

After leaving Bombay, Premchand decided to settle in Allahabad, where his sons, Sripat Rai and Amrit Rai were also studying. He also planned to publish *Hans* from there.

However, owing to his financial situation and constantly deteriorating health, he had to hand over *Hans* to the Indian Literary Counsel and move back to Benares.

Later, Premchand was elected as the first President of the Progressive Writers' Association in Lucknow, in 1936. *Godaan* (The Gift of a Cow), Premchand's last completed work, is considered his best work. Among the finest written novels in Hindi, the protagonist of *Godaan* is a poor peasant, who desperately longs for a cow, a symbol of wealth and prestige in rural India.

In 1936, Premchand also published *Kafan* (Shroud), which was the story of a poor man, who collects money for the funeral rites of his dead wife, but spends it on food and drink with his son instead.

ज़माना
क्रिकेट मैच
प्रेमचन्द

'Cricket Match,' Premchand's last story appeared in *Zamana* in 1938, after his death. He died on 8th October, 1936, after a prolonged sickness.

Unlike other contemporary renowned authors such as Rabindranath Tagore, Premchand was not appreciated much outside India, during his own lifetime. It was only after his death that many of his works were translated into English, Russian and other foreign languages.

OTHER TITLES IN THIS SERIES

OTHER TITLES IN THIS SERIES